SONS OF CALVIN
Three Huguenot Pastors

by

Alan C. Clifford

CHARENTON
Reformed Publishing

© Alan C. Clifford 1999

First published in Great Britain 1999
by Charenton Reformed Publishing
8 Le Strange Close, Norwich NR2 3PN

Typeset in Antiqua by
Charenton Reformed Publishing

British Library Cataloguing in Publication Data. A
catalogue record for this book is available from the
British Library.

Printed by Barkers Print and Design
Attleborough, Norfolk

ISBN 0 9526716 1 1

CONTENTS

LIST OF ILLUSTRATIONS

* Engraving by Samuel Bastide: with acknowledgements to the Collection Musée du Désert en Cévennes, France.

INTRODUCTION

Born at Noyon in Picardy, John Calvin (1509-64) is arguably the greatest Christian theologian of all time. Exiled from his native France, he became a pastor of the Church of Geneva and the organizing genius of the Protestant Reformation. While his Christ-exalting influence as a theologian, preacher and commentator was truly international, Calvin's labours were particularly fruitful in France. The comprehensive and clear Scriptural dynamism of the *Institutes of the Christian Religion*, the majesty and tenderness of the Genevan Psalter, the simplicity and reverence of the Reformed Liturgy and the practical directness of the Catechism gave the French Reformed churches a unique, powerful and godly character. Calvin's spirituality also found expression in the Confession of Faith and presbyterian Discipline of the French Reformed churches drawn up at the first National Synod held at Paris in 1559. Through the zealous evangelistic labours of pastors trained in Geneva, around 2,000 churches had been founded by 1560. Yet Huguenot piety was to be constantly tested through nearly three centuries of fierce persecution including the terrible St Bartholomew massacre of August 24, 1572. Cruelly harassed by the Roman Church, the noble army of French Reformed martyrs never failed to demonstrate the grace, electing love and faithfulness of the living God. Thus John Calvin's Bible-based, God-honouring legacy was constantly vindicated in the most inspiring epic of faith and fortitude ever known.

While Calvin's life and achievements are well known, the events and personalities of the French Reformation are mostly unknown, at least to the general Christian public. This is unfortunate since Calvin's influence on later generations of French Protestants is a truly inspiring story. Denied the joys of fatherhood - judged by his cruel critics as a sign of divine displeasure, Calvin's bold and prophetic response is famous: 'My sons are to be found all over the world.' However, this was not only true in his own day. Indeed, he had 'sons' in successive generations of whom it may be said that they too adopted Calvin's motto, 'I offer my heart to God as a sacrifice'. The following brief outlines of three eminent Huguenot pastors - not to ignore a little-known 'English son' - are presented to raise the profile of these and other servants of Christ whose dedicated labours for the Gospel deserve to be better known. In days of unparallelled apostasy and confusion within the professing Church, these Huguenot heroes challenge us to greater faithfulness and dedication to the cause of Christ. If this brief account contributes to that end then the author's enthusiasm for his subject will have been justified.

Further reading:

Benoit, J. - D., *Calvin in His Letters* (Abingdon, 1986).

John Calvin

Bouwsma, W. J., *John Calvin: a sixteenth-century portrait* (New York, 1988).

Cadier, J., *The Man God Mastered* (London, 1960).

McGrath, A., *A Life of John Calvin* (Oxford, 1990).

Parker, T. H. L., *John Calvin* (London, 1975).

Prestwich, M., (ed), *International Calvinism, 1541-1715* (Oxford, 1985).

Stickleberger, E., *Calvin* (London, 1959).

1

PREACHER *PAR EXCELLENCE*

Regarded by some as France's second Calvin, Jean Daillé, the famous Protestant preacher was born at Chatellerault (25 km north-east of Poitiers) on 6 January 1594. Growing up in a land ravaged by thirty years of religious wars, he was only four years old when the 'Calvinist-turned-Catholic' King Henry IV granted extensive liberties to his former Huguenot friends in the Edict of Nantes (1598). Dying in Paris in 1670, Jean Daillé thus lived and ministered during that period of fragile peace between the granting of the Edict and its revocation by King Louis XIV in 1685.

Observing Jean's great love for books, his father waived the idea of a business career for his son. At eleven years of age, he was sent to St Maixent in Poitou for his primary education. Bereaved early of parents who had suffered much for their Protestantism, an uncle became a diligent and devoted guardian, encouraging his nephew's spiritual stirrings.

GODLY SCHOLAR
Later Jean studied philosophy and theology at the

Jean Daillé

Reformed academy at Saumur, founded in 1599 by the town's governor, the eminent Huguenot soldier-statesman, Philippe Duplessis-Mornay (1549-1623). In recognition of his remarkable abilities, Daillé was appointed tutor to the governor's two grandsons in 1612. The governor - himself an accomplished scholar - was greatly attached to the future preacher on account of his youthful godliness. Spending many hours together, this protestant Gamaliel completed Daillé's education by imparting his solid biblical wisdom. In 1623 Daillé entered the ministry at M. Duplessis-Mornay's chateau of La Forêt-sur-Sèvre in lower Poitou. Shortly after, the Huguenot nobleman died in the arms of the new pastor who then assumed responsibility for the publication of his patron's memoirs.

POWERFUL PREACHER

Daillé's preaching and pastoral gifts were soon in great demand. In 1625 he was elected pastor of the Reformed church at Saumur. In the following year he was called by the Paris consistory to preach at the large temple at Charenton, where a congregation of several thousands was served by four or five pastors. From this influential centre of French Protestantism, Daillé ministered for forty-four years until his death in 1670. Published far and wide, his Christ-exalting sermons were appreciated for their clear exegesis, fervent delivery and warm application. Compared with his pastoral colleagues, it was said that Daillé was the only preacher whose voice could be clearly heard anywhere in the great temple. Very rarely absent from Charenton, he was a model of ministerial diligence. Daillé was thus regarded by many as the greatest French

Reformed preacher and author since John Calvin.

Living in troubled times, Daillé's earthly joys were tempered by national and personal tragedy. His only son Adrien was born on 31 October 1628. On that very day, after three unsuccessful relief attempts by the English navy, the besieged Protestant city of La Rochelle fell to Louis XIII's minister Cardinal Richelieu. That eventful day marked the end of political Protestantism in France. Inviting another comparison with Calvin, Daillé was bereaved of his devoted wife on 31 May 1631 after six years of marriage. He never remarried. Finding solace in the comforts of the Gospel and in greater literary activity, the Lord thus sanctified his servant's sorrows to the greater edification of the Reformed churches. Daillé was further comforted by a unique bond which developed between father and son. Trained by his father, Adrien was called to the pastorate of the Reformed church at La Rochelle in 1653. Following the death of his father's eminent colleague at Charenton, Jean Mestrezat (1592-1657), Adrien was called to serve alongside his father in 1658.

CONTENDER FOR THE FAITH
Besides his ever popular sermons, Daillé's books were in great demand. He brilliantly refuted Roman Catholic claims in *A Treatise Concerning the Right use of the Fathers* (1631) and *An Apology for the Reformed Churches* (1633). These works were deeply resented by the Roman clergy in France. Indeed, in the former work, the author makes nonsense of Rome's reliance on early patristic authority. Since disputes between

Rome and the Reformed churches involved theological developments of a much later date, e.g. transubstantiation became official only in 1215, the writings of the early fathers provided little help in resolving them. Besides, while dealing with other issues, many of their writings are forged, corrupted, obscure, mistaken, incompetent, self-contradictory and very far from being unanimous! In short, the writings of the Fathers have no place beside inspired and authoritative Scripture.

In the *Apology*, Daillé refutes the Roman charge that Protestants are schismatics, arguing that separation from her errors is an absolute necessity. While stating that differences between Reformed believers do not touch the foundation of faith, differences between Rome and the Reformed do. Drawing attention to the Roman doctrines of image worship, papal supremacy, tradition and the sacrifice of the mass, Daillé concludes: 'It is easy to see that these articles and many others...overthrow the foundations of faith and piety: so that it is not lawful for us to comply with those which hold them.'

When English translations of these works appeared, the Puritans rejoiced in the labours of their Huguenot brother. However, while Daillé's views on authority and churchmanship were welcomed by Presbyterians, many English Episcopalians were no less irritated than their French Roman Catholic counterparts. However, while none could doubt Daillé's strong Protestant convictions, moderate French Catholics held him in high esteem for his scholarship, abilities, integrity and wisdom. The Catholic *littérateur* J. - L. Guez de Balzac

(1597-1654) once exclaimed to him, "Oh that such a man as you are were on our side!"

AUTHENTIC CALVINIST

Daillé was also involved in internal debates among the Reformed churches. He agreed with his friend and former fellow-student, the Saumur academy Professor Moïse Amyraut (1596-1664) that the scholastic high Calvinism then in vogue was a distortion of John Calvin's more biblical teaching. Maliciously misrepresented ever since, the Amyraldians rejected a simplistic doctrine of limited atonement by appealing to the Bible, Calvin and the Canons of Dordt! Despite vindication at the two national Synods of Alençon (1637) and Charenton (1644), Amyraut was attacked by his high orthodox brethren in France and Holland. Attempting to pacify their anger, Daillé wrote in defense of the synods, continually warning that divisions among the Reformed could be exploited by Rome. He pleaded, "Do not set the house on fire to get rid of a spider!"

BRAVE AND LOYAL MODERATOR

During this critical mid-century period, Daillé's edifying ministry and wise counsel helped prepare the Reformed churches of France for the coming persecutions which, fifteen years after his death, culminated in the Revocation of the Edict of Nantes (1685). Always prominent in the national synods of the Reformed churches, he presided at the last synod prior to the revocation which assembled at Loudun in 1659. In his speech at the synod, the King's Commissioner demanded as usual that the Huguenots should be submissive to His Majesty and less antagonistic to the Church of Rome. While Daillé affirmed the loyalty and submission of the Reformed churches in all things lawful, he refused to dilute their theological stance. He bravely affirmed that, "As to those words *Antichrist*, found in our Liturgy, and *idolatry* and *deceit of Satan*, found in our Confession of Faith, they are the expressions that declare the reasons and the foundation of our separation from the Church of Rome, and the doctrine which our fathers maintained in the most cruel times, and which we are resolved, following their example, by God's grace, never to forsake, but to preserve faithfully and inviolably to the last moment of our lives."

COURAGEOUS PASTOR

Ever ready to contend for the faith, his personal courage was not confined to the printed page. In 1669, the last year of his life, Daillé was asked to attend the execution of a lapsed Protestant found guilty of murder. Refusing the services of a priest, the man's request for a Protestant pastor was granted by the judge. Sentenced to breaking on the wheel, thousands of noisy Roman Catholics were present to witness the awful spectacle. Seizing the opportunity to preach the Gospel, Daillé courageously made his way to the scaffold. His compassionate ministrations before the now silent Parisian mob happily brought the poor wretch to repentance and faith in Christ. Lifting up his powerful voice in prayer, Daillé commended the saved sinner to God as the dreadful sentence was carried out. Undisturbed by the subdued and thoughtful crowd, he then descended the scaffold and returned safely to his house.

Shortly after this incident, the eldest of Daillé's four colleagues, Charles Drelincourt (1595-1669) died. In the following spring, having prepared his Easter sermons, Daillé seemingly suffered a stroke. He lingered for several days, during which he frequently uttered the words, 'For me to live is Christ and to die is gain'. After commending his family and friends to God, he died on 15 April 1670, aged 76 years.

ELOQUENT EXPOSITOR
The warm and experimental Reformed Christianity of Daillé's *Expositions of Philippians* (1643) and *Colossians* (1648) was immensly appreciated on this side of the Channel. Last published in the UK by James Nichol (Edinburgh, 1863), the Huguenot preacher's sermons have never failed to instruct and inspire. Daillé's Nichol series editor James Sherman (1796-1862, formerly minister of Castle Street Chapel, Reading and the Surrey Chapel, London) quotes an unnamed 'devoted servant of Christ' who had written on his copy of the 1672 edition, 'This is the most eloquent book in my library'. In the eighteenth century, Henry Venn wrote to his son of the reviving influence of Daillé's sermons: "This last week has been very gloomy, cold, misty weather: we have not had one visitor; but I have enjoyed a feast, in reading M. Daillé on the Colossians. What a judicious writer! What a masterly expositor! The truth, the fulness of Christ, are so set forth by him, as to make my heart glow; and I am the better for what I read."

James Sherman's own commendation of Daillé's sermons is impressive: 'They are marked by clear interpretation of Scripture - great candour towards other expositors - boldness for the faith - and vigorous attacks on the errors of the papacy, which he exposes with singular skill, and refutes with masculine energy. His sanctified eloquence appears in every page, but especially in his perorations, which for close appeals to the conscience, ardent love to a precious Saviour, earnest exhortations to holy walking with God, and active service for Christ, exceed any which have fallen into the editor's hands...' Somewhat less striking, C. H. Spurgeon's brief remark on Daillé's expositions is not to be ignored: 'Written in a deliciously florid style. Very sweet and evangelical: after the French manner'.

A recent commendation justifies continuing interest in Daillé. Dr Cyril J. Barber writes in the Klock & Klock facsimile edition (1983) of Daillé's *Colossians*: 'In contrast to some puritan works of this period, Daillé adhered more closely to the text of Scripture, expounded each verse fully, and generally leaves his readers astonished at his wisdom and insight.'

It is surely fitting to allow this prince of Huguenot preachers the last word - or shall we say 'words'? The following extracts perfectly illustrate those evangelical virtues for which Daillé's sermons were famous.

As Sherman correctly remarks, Daillé robustly refuted the claims of the Church of Rome. Indeed, he was not slow to defend the Reformed Faith on the grounds that Roman teaching consisted of post-apostolic novelties:

'Whence we may deduce, as we pass on, an invincible proof, both of the truth of the doctrine which we believe, and of the vanity of that which we contest with our adversaries of Rome. For as to what we hold, it is evident that the apostles taught it in all the world, both by word of mouth and by writing, as all the necessary, positive, and affirmative articles of our faith fully appear in the monuments of apostolic preaching; that is, both in the books which they wrote, and in the churches they founded. As for our adversaries, it is no less evident that they can never show that the monarchy or infallibility of their pope, or the adoration of their host, or the service of their images, or the invocation of their saints, or purgatory, or the traffic of their indulgences, or any other of the points which we debate with them, was preached in all the world at the time of the holy apostle. Not a single trace of them can be found in any of the books or memorials remaining of that age, or of a long time beyond it; only a man may perceive them, some ages after, growing up, one in one place and another in another, at various times and in different regions; an evident sign that they are not parts of the gospel of Jesus Christ, which was fully preached in all the world in St Paul's lifetime, but the inventions and traditions of men that have arrived since' (*Sermon on Colossians 1:6-8*).

Needless to say, Daillé - like Luther, Calvin and all the reformers - gloried in the atoning, substitutionary death of our Lord Jesus Christ as the only foundation of the sinner's justification and salvation before God. How are sinners counted righteous before God? 'All in virtue of that obedience which Jesus rendered to the Father on the cross, where he was made sin and a curse for us, his agonies being imputed to us as though we had suffered them'. Truly, God communicates the righteousness of faith 'in imputing to the believer the obedience of the Mediator, regarding him with a favourable eye when thus clothed as it were with Jesus, and crowning him with all the benefits he purchased by his death upon the cross' *(Sermon on Philippians 3:9-11)*.

As in the sixteenth century, Daillé and his brethren of the seventeenth had to rebut Rome's accusations that the Reformed doctrine of justification produced moral laxity: 'And in this our day, is not our doctrine misunderstood and calumniated in the same way? Do they not say, since you are justified by faith alone, what inducement have you to perform good works? But, O ye adversaries it is to perform good works that I am justified. This divine righteousness of Christ has been communicated to me, in order that I may be transformed into his image; that I may know the power of his resurrection, and that I may be like him, a new creature; that I may love God, not to lay him under obligation to me, (far, far from my soul such a preposterous notion) but to acquit myself in a small degree of the immense debt I owe him. I love him because he has loved me, because God is love, and because he has sent his Son Jesus to die and rise again for me. Will my obedience be less acceptable to him because I think not of merit in rendering it? Will he reject it because the cross and resurrection of Christ inspires it, and not an intention of deserving a reward?...Why may I not serve God here on earth in the same manner as I hope to serve him hereafter in heaven, with a pure, a free, and truly filial affection? And such affection, far from presuming to acquire any right or reward from so good and so merciful a Father, must after all its efforts remain dissatisfied with itself, and be content to ascribe all it has been able to do to his free grace alone' *(Sermon on Philippians 3:9-11).*

As one might expect, Daillé traces our salvation by 'free grace alone' back to sovereign, divine election. Christians 'have the honour to be elected of God, the saints, and the beloved of God'. Accordingly, 'The election of God is the choice which he makes, according to his good pleasure, of certain persons, to call them to the knowledge of himself, and the glory of his salvation. And this term, election, signifies sometimes the resolution he has taken in his eternal counsel to choose and call them, which Scripture elsewhere calls the determinate purpose of God, Eph. 1:11' *(Sermon on Colossians 3:12-13).*

As with Calvin, Amyraut *and* the Canons of Dordt, Daillé is not paralysed by the decree of God into suppressing the free offer of the gospel. He resists the scholastic rationalism of the day in not explaining away the universality of the gospel: 'For although [Christ] 'is the propitiation for the sins of the whole world', 1 John 2:2, and the worth of his sacrifice so great that it abundantly suffices to expiate all the crimes of the universe; and although the salvation obtained by him is really offered, and by his will, unto all men yet none actually enjoy it but those that enter into his communion by faith, and are by that means in him, as that clause of his covenant expressly imports, 'God so loved the world, that he gave his only begotten Son, that whosoever believeth in him should not perish, but have everlasting life,' John 3:16' *(Sermon on Colossians 1:14)*.

For Daillé, the doctrine and experience of the gospel produces holiness and purity of life. It also produces joy and assurance in the believer's heart, notwithstanding the trials of this life:

'Rejoice, then, believing souls, in your Divine Redeemer. Drown every care in these sweet reflections:...In this case you will never [lack] a subject of rejoicing. For you perceive the apostle commands you to be always joyful: "Rejoice in the Lord always;" and, as if he were immediately in a transport of joy himself, he adds, "and again I say rejoice." Listen not to the flesh, which now whispers in your ear that this may be very well for the day of prosperity; but that in the season of affliction, when bending beneath the cross, when sickness weakens, when losses afflict, or when persecution presses hard, it would then be out of season then to say "Rejoice." The flesh, brethren, comprehends not this mystery; it surpasses its sense and understanding. The joy of the Lord is unlike that of the world, which the vapours of the earth extinguish, which is easily overturned by the casualties of life; the joy of Christ is eternal; it maintains itself against everything; nothing can extinguish it; it lives even in the furnace of affliction; and triumphs over death itself' *(Sermon on Philippians 4:4-7)*.

Daillé knew how to be pastorally practical, not least where sickness and suffering were concerned:

'Never let the illnesses with which God visits us either make us doubt his love or our election. He has truly promised us in this world his friendship, his peace, the joy of his Spirit, and the assistance of his Christ, and in another immortality. But he nowhere promises that we shall be exempted from the evils and miseries of the present life. He declares to us on the contrary, that we shall be more subject to them than others. Let us then receive these strokes from his hand with patience and gentleness of mind, and instead of murmuring or hardening ourselves under the rod, let us profit by it as a salutary correction and an honourable trial, learning from it the vanity of this life, and of all the good that it possesses, thinking rightly of the infirmity of our nature, and of death, which will assuredly destroy it, to withdraw our affections from earth, to renounce vice and its lusts, and to aspire only after a blessed immortality, the end and prize of our holy calling. And as to your life, if it is useful, either to the church or to your families, I do not forbid that you desire it; I simply wish that you would ask it from God, and expect it from his mercy alone, who brings to the tomb, and lifts you from it, when he will; and that, when you have recovered your health, you would ascribe to his goodness all the glory of your cure, devoutly consecrating to his service all the fruits of a life which you only hold from his grace' (*Sermon on Philippians 2:25-30*).

It is impossible to do justice to Daillé's preaching in a few extracts. Suffice to say that on every branch of doctrinal, experiental and practical Christianity, his expository skills justify the reputation he acquired in his lifetime. The two volumes of published sermons in English invite one to hope that the many French volumes deposited in Geneva might one day also appear in English. We conclude with Daillé's eloquent encouragement to the pilgrim people of God:

'We have a part in the heritage of the saints. The kingdom of the beloved Son of God has been given us. O great and magnificent portion! Let the world boast of and adore its gold, its honours, and its delights, as much as it pleases; we have that better part, which is sufficient to make us eternally happy, though we should be deprived of all other things. Christian, if the world were to bereave you of what you have within its jurisdiction, consider, it cannot take from you the inheritance of the saints. If it denies you its leeks, and onions, and flesh-pots, it cannot debar you from that Divine light which shines on you, and which, in spite of all its attempts, will conduct you to your blissful Canaan. If it takes from you its honours, should it drive you even out of its dominions, it will not be able to wrest from you the kingdom of the Son of God, nor the dignity and glory you possess in it. This is not a corruptible kingdom; it is not like those of the earth, that are subject to a thousand and a thousand dishonours, miseries, and mutations. It is an immortal kingdom, firmer than the heavens; so abundant in glory and in goodness, that it changes all those who partake of it into kings and priests. Faithful brethren, let us be contented with so advantageous a portion. Let us enjoy it for the present by a lively and established hope, meekly bearing the inconveniences of this brief journey we are taking to attain it, and patiently expect that blessed day, when our heavenly Father, having finished the work of his grace, will elevate us all into his glory, and put on our heads the crowns of life and immortality, which he has promised us in the eternal communion of his well-beloved Son. To whom, with the Father and the Holy Spirit, the true and only God, blessed for ever, be all honour and praise, for ever and ever. Amen' *(Sermon on Colossians 1:12-13).*

Further reading:

Baird, H. M., *The Huguenots and the Revocation of the Edict of Nantes,* 2 vols (London , 1895).
Bayle, P., *Dictionary Historical and Critical* (London, 1735), Vol. 2 (article under 'Daillé').
Clifford, A. C., *Calvinus: authentic Calvinism, a clarification* (Norwich, 1996).
Daillé, J., *Exposition of Philippians and Colossians* (Edinburgh, 1863).
Quick, J., *Icones Sacrae Gallicanae* (1700), MS on deposit at Dr Williams's Library, London , DWL 6. 38-39 (39).
Van Stam, F. P., *The Controversy over the Theology of Saumur, 1635-1650* (Amsterdam & Maarssen, 1988).

2

A TALE OF TWO PASTORS:

JOHN QUICK AND CLAUDE BROUSSON

The final decade of the twentieth century supplied a feast of anniversaries. In the context of European Reformed Protestantism, 1998 did not pass without recalling the quatercentenery of the Edict of Nantes (1598), that early experiment in religious toleration in France, cruelly revoked by Louis XIV in 1685. 1998 was also the tercentenary of the martyrdom of arguably Europe's greatest ever pastor-evangelist, the French Huguenot Claude Brousson, himself a victim of the revocation of the Edict of Nantes. These events linked up with the earlier 'bibliographical tercentenery' of a little-known work intimately related to the above events. Of course, the year 1992 provided a series of significant anniversaries: we remembered the discovery of America by Christopher Columbus (1492) and the commencement of the English Civil War (1642). Of more immediate interest to evangelical Christians was William Carey's zealous involvement in the dawn of

John Quick

modern missions (1792) and the home-call of Charles Haddon Spurgeon (1892). If the importance of such events is incontestible, how could the publication of a little-known book have justified our attention? For the friends of the Reformed Faith, its noble and evocative title-page surely explains why: '*SYNODICON IN GALLIA REFORMATA: or the Acts, Decisions, Decrees, and Canons of those famous National Councils of the Reformed Churches in France...Being a most faithful and impartial history of the rise, growth, perfection and decay of the Reformation in that kingdom, with its fatal catastrophe upon the Revocation of the Edict of Nantes, in the year 1685...A record of very many illustrious events of divine providence relating to those churches...The whole collected and composed out of original manuscript acts of those renowned Synods...A work never before extant in any language...In Two Volumes...by John Quick, Minister of the Gospel in London ...(1692)'*.

The author of these fascinating folios was a little-known Presbyterian minister from the west of England. John Quick was born at Plymouth in 1636. After graduating at Oxford in 1657 he was ordained at Ermington in Devon in 1659. Along with his illustrious puritan brethren - a more famous contemporary John Flavel (1628-91) ministered at nearby Dartmouth, Quick exercised a faithful and courageous ministry. He served at Kingsbridge with Churchstow and then at Brixton near Plymouth. Undeterred by the Act of Uniformity (1662), he continued to preach. He was arrested during the Lord's Day morning worship on 13 December 1663 and imprisoned at Exeter. At his trial, he was nearly acquitted on a technicality. However, since he refused to give up preaching, he was sent to prison. After suffering for a further eight weeks, he was liberated by Sir Matthew Hale. The Bishop of Exeter, Seth Ward then prosecuted Quick for preaching to the prisoners but the Lord's servant was acquitted, his unashamed 'guilt' notwithstanding!

Charles II's Indulgence of 1672 brought a brief respite for the persecuted puritan brotherhood. Quick was licensed to preach at Plymouth. When restrictions were imposed again the following year, he was imprisoned for three months with other nonconformists at the Marshalsea prison in Plymouth. On his release, Quick left the west of England for London. He then travelled to Holland where he became a minister to the English church at Middleburg in 1679. Returning to London two years later, Quick gathered a Presbyterian congregation in a small meeting house in Middlesex Court, Bartholomew Close, Smithfield. On the eve of easier times, his London ministry - 'successful to the conversion of many', says Dr Edmund Calamy - was relatively undisturbed; the 'Glorious Revolution' and the Toleration Act of 1689 eventually brought persecution to an end. Known as 'a serious, good preacher' with a 'great facility and freedom in prayer', John Quick continued to serve his people faithfully until his death on 29 April 1706. His wife Elizabeth died in 1708. Their only daughter became the wife of Dr John Evans (1680?-1730) who completed the commentary on the Epistle to the Romans in Matthew Henry's immortal *Exposition*.

Consistent with his personal courage and pastoral

gifts, John Quick combined scholarship with zeal for the truth. The blending of these qualities explains his authorship of the *Synodicon in Gallia Reformata*. During his early ministry and subsequently, he became acquainted with the Huguenot refugees, some of whom landed at his native Plymouth from La Rochelle in 1681 - the year the dreadful 'dragonnades' began. Accordingly, writes Calamy, Quick 'was very compassionate to those in distress; at a great deal of pains and expense for the relief of the poor French Protestants, and his house and purse were almost ever open to them. He was a perfect master of their language, and had a peculiar respect for their churches, upon the account of their sound doctrine and useful discipline, and the noble testimony which they bore to religion by their sufferings'.

Quick's interest in the Huguenots did not end with the *Synodicon*. Besides a few published sermons of his own, he also prepared for publication a selection of fifty brief (some quite lengthy) biographies of eminent pastors, theologians and martyrs of the French Reformed Church, the *Icones Sacrae Gallicanae*. He also produced a similar selection of twenty Puritans, the *Icones Sacrae Anglicanae*. These ambitious ventures failed with the death in 1700 of William Russell, Duke of Bedford (the dedicatee of the *Synodicon*) who had offered to assist with the cost. Advancing illness also prevented Quick from collecting subscriptions for the work. Following the author's death, the manuscript volumes were eventually deposited at Dr Williams's Library in London.

Claude Brousson

ELOQUENT LAWYER

This brings us to the final biography in the French *Icones*, that of the famous martyr Claude Brousson. Born at Nîmes in 1647, Brousson was trained for the bar, serving eventually as an advocate at Toulouse. He frequently defended Protestants with great eloquence against the ever worsening legal enactments issued against them by the Jesuit-inspired policies of King Louis XIV. His life and freedom threatened by the Roman Catholic authorities, Brousson fled to Lausanne. With their temples demolished and the flocks scattered, the mounting persecutions of Reformed believers following the Revocation of the Edict of Nantes in 1685 filled him with distress. After visiting Berlin and Amsterdam to arouse support for the persecuted - and in the face of antagonism from refugee pastors he had criticized for leaving their flocks, Brousson felt the call of God to return to France, not as a lawyer but as a pastor. Returning to the Cévennes in the summer of 1689, he commenced one of the most courageous and sacrificial ministries in the history of the Christian church. His heart bled with Christ-like compassion for pastorless souls who, under the most diabolical pressures of persecution had, in considerable numbers, abjured their faith.

Living with constant danger, exhaustion, deprivation and the discomforts of cave and forest-dwelling in climatic extremes, Brousson's itinerant ministry to the 'churches of the desert' was phenomenal by apostolic standards. Interrupted by recuperative and support-raising visits to Switzerland, Germany and England,

and a brief pastorate in Holland, Brousson's labours ended during his third and final visit to France which began in August 1697. Leaving his family at the Hague, the fears of his tearful wife were now to be realised. He was betrayed and arrested near Pau in south-western France and imprisoned in the Citadel at Montpellier on 30 October 1698. His execution on 4 November proved a glorious demonstration of the all-sufficient grace of God. After the martyrdom of this remarkable servant of Christ, the Montpellier executioner declared, "I have put to death two hundred convicts, but none have ever made me tremble like M. Brousson."

John Quick's biography of Claude Brousson is noteworthy in several respects, not least because in 1694 a personal meeting took place between author and subject during Brousson's visit to England. Writing in 1700, Quick says of his Huguenot hero:

I had the honour of his acquaintance and was favoured with a conversation with him in my house [in Bunhill Fields] about seven years ago, when he was in London, which lasted five good hours. The time seemed very short unto me, that I was blessed with such a guest...We spent the time in Christian conference and discourse...Not a vain or idle word dropped from his mouth. He seemed an angel in a human body, who was not content to go to heaven alone, but would carry his friends, countrymen and strangers thither together with him also.

Quick's epic account of Brousson's heroic ministry must rank with the most vivid and inspiring Christian literature ever written. From this little known MS material, the following carefully chosen extracts portray Brousson's personal godliness, pastoral zeal and sacrificial dedication to the cause of Christ in the midst of the most horrific, ruthless and brutal persecution of the period. Despite the most determined opposition, his activities and experiences remain unique examples of the all-sufficient and sustaining grace of the living God.

ZEALOUS PASTOR

Broussons's pastoral labours probably have no parallel in the seventeenth century. In the English-speaking world, even the work of Richard Baxter is not on the same scale. Furthermore, at a time when English Nonconformity was becoming notorious for doctrinal decay and moribund spirituality, Brousson displayed the zeal of purer times. Fifty years before the Methodist Revival, Brousson's itinerant activities anticipated those of Whitefield and the Wesleys, the Huguenot's being conducted in far more hostile conditions. John Quick continues the story:

In the Cévennes and Lower Languedoc...there were quartered...several regiments of dragoons who rode up and down night and day to hinder all religious meetings; and yet notwithstanding all their pains, subtlety and malice, they were both very frequent and numerous. Every night there was one or more of these assemblies celebrated for divine service; for ordinarily they met at midnight. M. Brousson the first two years of his ministry held very many of them, at least three or four every week, till by the unseasonableness of the time (which in nature was designed for rest) and the

*overstraining of his lungs in speaking, he quite broke his
health, and contracted such a soreness in his breast, as he
could never be rid of it to his dying day.*

*The desolation of the people of God was deplorable. This
grieved his very soul. For they being as sheep without a
shepherd were every moment exposed to the fury and malice
of those evening wolves and ravening bears, the idolatrous
priests of the Romish synagogue who shewed them no
mercy, but most insatiably worried and devoured them.
When he reposed himself a little while, he was necessitated
to range over a wild and spacious country to exercise in
other assemblies. Sometimes the meetings were nearer,
other times at farther distance, according as they could find
a conveniency to be together.*

*Before he could tarry at one place a week, he was necessitated
upon times to preach ten, twelve, fifteen and once five and
twenty sermons at these meetings in the space of eight days.
These were indeed the labours of a true apostle of our Lord.
For a fortnight together he hath preached every other night;
transporting himself that evening in which he did not
preach unto the next place appointed for that service. At
ordinary meetings he was obliged to speak three hours, and
in those of them that the Lord's Supper was administered,
no less than four or four and a half. The most of which time
was spent in prayer, because of the doleful calamities of
God's poor Zion in France. One thing, though it much
comforted him, was yet no mean affliction to him, and a
mighty prejudice unto his voice. It was this; he was
necessitated to raise all the psalms, and to guide all the
people himself, that they might sing musically. And the*

[34]

tunes of the French Psalms as they are most sweet and melodious, so many of them are of very high and lofty notes, to the true singing of which there is required sound lungs, and a clear strong voice. This made him strain his lungs, and put his voice and breast upon the rack. But he was the servant of God and his Church, and he valued not his health, nor counted his life dear unto him, so that he might serve and save souls, fulfil the ministry unto which he was called, and finish his course with joy.

After the sermons were ended, he usually made a plain and familiar discourse, in which he exhorted those who by reason of the violence of temptation, and frailty of human nature had fallen from their holy profession, to repent heartily and enter the bosom of the church unfeignedly, and to renounce all the reigning sins of this present age, and the abominations of unclean Babylon, and to swear allegiance and fidelity unto God, and to keep his commandments diligently for the future. And the Lord crowned this exercise with a rare and wonderful blessing. For I remember in those five hours conversation with him in my house, he told me that in one part only of one of the western provinces of France, no fewer than five thousand persons kneeling down upon the bare ground with streaming tears, deep sighs and heart cutting groans, after such familiar exhortations of his, did most bitterly lament their revolt from our holy religion, and with eyes and hands lifted up to heaven did call God to witness upon their souls that they renounced the Romish faith, worship and discipline, that they would never any more have or hold communion with that idolatrous antichristian synagogue, that they would never bow the knee to Baal more, never go to mass, come what there would of it, and that they would hold fast the profession of their faith, and the true religion through the grace of God without wavering, and persevere immovably in it unto the end. This I say was in only one part of a province. But he had reclaimed some thousands more in other provinces. So mighty was the power and presence of God with him in his ministry. He never baptized infants in the larger but lesser assemblies.

Over and besides these labours in their solemn meetings, M. Brousson spent three hours every day in prayer, the first in the morning, the second at three in the afternoon, the third in the evening, for the comfort of those families where he stopped or lodged, as he travelled from one place unto another, or that took upon them the care of his person, and watched for his preservation, or of the faithful who assisted at these holy exercises. He most usually accompanied these prayers with a most lively exhortation unto those who were present at them. He preached twice every Lord's Day, in the morning and afternoon; besides he repeated his sermons unto such of the faithful, as knowing the place of his retreat, would visit him in the evening.

Nor did he preach the Gospel by word of mouth but did it also by writing. For in those nights in which there were no assemblies, he sat up transcribing copies of his sermons which he sent abroad among the godly, and the subject matter of which were the most important points of Christianity, such as were of indispensible necessity to be known that we might be saved...All his sermons were written in a becoming plainness, suited to the capacity of his auditors and in the divine style of the Sacred Scripture, in the heavenly language which the Holy Ghost taught the divinely inspired prophets, evangelists and apostles to hand down unto us their infallible oracles, books, gospels and epistles. So that through the grace of God he delivered the celestial doctrine in its natural simplicity, purity and evidence: whereby that poor people were wonderfully edified. These little sermons of his took with them most mightily, and 'twas who could purchase them, especially in those places where there were no assemblies nor ministers. To this purpose he always carried with him a little desk to write upon, and which he placed upon his knees when he wrote, and the godly in the Cévennes and Lower Languedoc called 'the table in the wilderness'. So that when his impaired health, and the infernal rage of his enemies hindered and took him off from preaching in the wilderness meetings, yet God granted him this consolation that by his written sermons he preached louder, and was heard at a farther distance, than if he had uttered them before a particular congregation.

M. Brousson also did at several reprises contend by other writings in defense of the truth. These were the results of his spare hours, when against his will he had an extraordinary vacation. These he dispatched unto the court at Versailles. Such was his Apology for the Project of the Reformed in France, and for those other Servants of God who preached and assembled to worship God in that forlorne kingdom. But God the most righteous judge as he hardened Pharoah and the heart of the Egyptians his subjects, so did God harden the heart of the French king, of the sycophants his counsellors, and of his sodomitical clergy, so that they would not let the Protestants go free to serve and worship

Him, nor to pay unto the Divine Majesty those homages which are due unto Him from men and angels. Yea the task of bricks hath been since doubled and trebled, as the zealous affection of His poor people augmented to follow him in the wilderness there to adore and hold communion with Him. Hence they turned every stone, and tried all kinds of experiments utterly to destroy those few ministers who laboured to instruct and comfort them.

Over and above those five regiments of dragoons before mentioned maintained and dispersed by the clergy in the Cévennes and Lower Languedoc to keep the good people from worshipping God according to His appointments, there were also several garrisons in those two provinces in the forts of Alès, St Hippolyte and at Nîmes. These made it their incessant business either to seize upon or massacre the poor ministers of the word, but their principal aim was at [François] Vivens and Brousson. So that in the year 1691, an ordinance was published in which they promised 5000 livres to him or them, that should take either of these servants of God alive or dead. Thus had anyone liberty to murder them, and those assassins that should make them away were sure of a rich reward from the Government...

BRUTAL PERSECUTION
Like the English Puritans and the Scottish Covenanters, the French Huguenots also had their episodes of military conflict. Whether or not Christians should ever resort to the sword in the face of persecution and despotism is a question of timeless importance. In an atmosphere of relentless provocation, graphically related by Quick, Brousson's teaching and example pos-

sess a unique challenge. Its relevance to current discussion cannot be ignored:

But the faithful in the Cévennes being most cruelly oppressed, as yet they are to this very day [1700], it was impossible but that some persons transported with a blind zeal or by the motions of their natural choler which they could not always master, should break out into intemperate actions or expressions, especially when as they saw their nearest relations murdered before their faces without any legal trial, only for serving God. M. Brousson did not approve of such transports and restrained them to the utmost of his power. But sometimes he had to do with men whose spirits were so embittered by reason of those manifold evils they suffered that they grew stark desperate. They would complain, and they had too just and too much ground to complain, that the Edicts most religiously sworn to them were violated, all Treaties of Pacification rescinded, that the most barbarous hostilities were exercised towards the Reformed, that they were against their consciences compelled to abjure the true religion by which they hoped for salvation. They were cruelly tortured in their bodies, plundered of their goods, racked in their consciences, and all for no crime in. the least but this, that they kept the commandments of God and therefore they were as sheep devoted to the slaughter and massacred every day.

In Poitou, in Lower Languedoc, in the Cévennes, [the dragoons] had perpetrated already numberless massacres. And if they had not committed murders enough upon Protestants, they fell foul again upon them. One of the ladies of Belcastell received a deep wound in her head with a cutlass. *Many of the faithful were killed at a meeting nigh unto St Germain in the Cévennes and a greater number of them wounded, and divers attempting to save themselves were drowned. This was in June 1686. The July following, a great multitude of them as they were at the worship of God about two leagues from Uzès were most of them slaughtered in the very place. The popish dragoons mingled their blood with their sacrifices. Some of both sexes were taken and hanged up immediately. In October of the same year, 40 persons more for the same heinous crime in meeting together to call upon God were all of them shot dead at Le Vigan in the Cévennes. In the month of February 1689, no fewer than 300 souls were butchered in the place of meeting which was on another mountain of Vivarais, and they cut the throats of about 50 more in the Vaunage. It was that monster of a man (and surely the African monsters were more humane than he) the Intendant Bâsville that did by express orders enjoin these unheard of murders. His dragoons soaked in blood spared neither sex or age, but slew all, young, old, men, women and sucking children indifferently. When the murderers came and assaulted these innocent lambs, they were all at prayer, upon their knees, with their eyes and hands lifted up to heaven; and in this very posture did they kill them either with their carbines or sabres. Yea many of them did open their own breasts voluntarily to receive the mortal shot or blow from them, rather than they would abjure their religion.*

One of these dragoons, a worthy apostle of that old red dragon murdered a poor woman, whose little infant was sucking at her breast; and coming up to her, the poor babe smiling upon him held out its pretty hand to play with him.

[40]

But instead of playing with it, this devil incarnate stabbeth this poor lamb with his bayonet into the heart, and holding it up, crieth unto his comrade, "See, see", saith he, "how this frog which I have stuck yet sprawleth!" When the Intendant Bâsville was informed of this horrible murder, he takes no notice of it, but only asked the murderer whether the woman had any other children. And he answering yes, "Well", quoth he, "'tis so much the worse for thee. For one time or other they will avenge their mother's death upon thee..."

Had these poor Christians the patience of angels, they could hardly have born up without resenting of such barbarous inhumanities. Yea, although they found any of the faithful quiet at home, nor at any of these meetings, if they had not their throats cut, yet they were robbed and spoiled of all their goods, their homes demolished, their families dissipated, and the men, as if they had been the most incorrigible villains in nature were condemned unto the galleys. These violences, these murders and massacres made many very sober persons contrary to their former resolutions to grow impatient.

Now though the injustice and cruelty of these bloody persecutions exceeded all bounds, yet M. Brousson could not approve of [François Vivens' violent retaliation against the dragoons] which proceeded from a mistaken and immoderate zeal. His enemies proclaimed open war against him, and he bade defiance unto them. M. Brousson did frequently represent unto him, that the weapons of our warfare are spiritual, and that he should use none other sword but the sword of the Spirit...that is to say the Gospel shall be preached with a spirit of sweetness and love, and it will be by this means, that God will convert the nations and will perfectly set up His kingdom in the whole world. This very doctrine did M. Brousson oftentimes inculcate unto his brother Vivens and to some other Protestants who were acted by the same spirit of fire, zeal and indignation.

DIVINE AID

Much of Reformed theology's oft-lamented reputation for sterile orthodoxy has its origins in the seventeenth century. Such cerebralism, so it is argued, justifed the warmth and 'enthusiasm' of the Methodist Revival. According to Quick's account, Brousson was far removed from the Dutch and Anglo-Saxon Reformed stereotype. When clinically accurate theology would have been meagre sustenance indeed, Brousson's experiences of the Holy Spirit reveal a higher dimension. He was favoured with an extraordinary assurance, the details of which invite a comparison with the experiences enjoyed by eighteenth-century Methodists in far less threatening circumstances:

Now although M. Brousson was like unto a pelican in the wilderness and an owl in the desert, and forced to lurk in caves and dens of the earth, yet was he continually pursued by his enemies. Which way soever he turned his head he could see nothing else but death before him, yea that death which was most cruel. For the Government was much more exasperated against him than against all the other servants of God. But he was wonderfully supported by divine grace. A thousand times hath he concluded with himself, "All way of escape faileth, I shall certainly now be taken, I cannot but fall into the hands of these Sauls." Infinite times hath he looked martyrdom in the face, and he hath resigned up his soul to God as if the sentence of death were the very next moment to be executed upon him.

Sometimes the Lord hath dawned in with a beam of hope into his heart, and then he would persuade himself that God would never suffer him to fall into his enemy's hands, that He would never sell nor deliver him up to those cruel oppressors, that thirsted for his blood, and prepared for him the most exquisite and unheard of torments. But a while after, he fell into his old fears, darkness and terrible alarms. Insomuch that it was even with him as with Job and David, he was scared with visions and terrified with dreams. Yet recollecting himself and the carriage of divine providence towards him, he would say unto his soul, "Why art thou cast down O my soul? Why art thou disquieted within me? Hope still in God, who is the light of thy countenance and thy God. My life is in His hands. If He will have me die, 'tis not all the world can hinder it. And if I must die, 'tis better dying in the way of duty than in the neglect of it." Whereupon he went and preached the Gospel in those places where he had promised. And the danger was visible, yet the wisdom and mercy of God safeguarded him. He was in the midst of a burning furnace which was heated against him seven times hotter than usual, but the providence of God did most miraculously preserve him...

Now and then M. Brousson might get a soft bed at Nîmes, but his ordinary lodging was in the woods, on the mountains, in dens and caves of the earth. He was royally accommodated when he had sweet fresh straw; at other times he must be contented to lie on a dunghill, or upon fagots, to sleep under a tree, under bushes, in the clefts of rocks, and

*under ground in holes of the earth. In the summer he was
consumed with the burning heat of the sun. In the winter
he was almost frozen to death upon the cold mountains of ice
and snow, not daring to kindle a fire to warm him for fear
the smoke or light thereof should discover him, nor durst he
get out of his hiding place to enjoy the comfort of the warm
sun lest he should be seen by his enemies and false brethren.
Many times hath he been pinched with hunger, wanting
food to sustain nature, and was fainting away for want of
drink. The fatigues that he has endured have brought him so
low that he hath been next door to the grave. Wherefore in
all those pictures of him which were scattered up and down
the kingdom in city and country, in order to his discovery,
he was represented as a man of a sallow countenance, tanned
with the sun, exceeding thin, and meagre as a skeleton. Yet
did none of these things grieve him when he considered that
he suffered them in God's service, for His glory and the
consolation of his poor people.*

*And when this poor people considered the calamities and
dangers to which he was incessantly exposed in his labours
for the salvation of their souls, and when they also reflected
upon the innocency of his life and that grace of God given
him to preach His word in its native simplicity and purity,
in the evidence and demonstration of the Spirit, he never
retired from those holy meetings but that several of them
would fall upon his neck, kiss him and wish a thousand
blessings upon him. Moreover the Lord led him into His
banqueting house, displayed the banner of His love over
him, made him taste those joys of the Holy Ghost, which are
unspeakably sweet, ravishing and full of glory. But he felt
those heavenly consolations in his soul mostly when he was*

preaching or praying in those holy assemblies or administering the Lord's Supper. Then was he stayed with flagons of new wine of the heavenly kingdom; then was he comforted with the apples of the celestial paradise. He was even sick with the love of God, the glories thereof overflowing his feeble nature. Christ's left hand was under his head and His right hand did embrace him.

He had one experience, yet he believed that it was not his own only, but that other servants of God might sense it as well as himself, that although he was environed with armies of enemies, who coursed up and down continually in search of him, yet no sooner was he got into those holy assemblies and had lifted up his heart to God in prayer or had opened his mouth to sing His praises or to preach His word, but that all his carnal servile fears vanished and his mind was as quiet, serene and calm as if he had been in a land of liberty. And he had this great tranquillity of soul whenever he took pen in hand to write in behalf of the truth, for the advancement of God's kingdom and the consolation of His desolate church. He composed also in the midst of these pressing dangers several pieces which are since published and which he sent to Court for the justifying of that doctrine which he preached. This cannot but be wondered at. But God magnified His own glorious power in the weakness of His instrument...

From the year 1692, M. Brousson set up those holy meetings again; but his breast was so very sore that he could only preach but once in seven days. Yet was not the people's zeal allayed during his long indisposition. For that taste they had of the sweet and heavenly comforts of the Holy Ghost, and their fear of losing them, the many copies of his sermons,

letters and prayers which he had dispersed among them,
which falling into the hands of persons of quality and of estate
in the world, it raised up such a flame in their souls after the
word of God, that now rich merchants, noble gentlemen, lords
and ladies with their families and children, who were formerly
lukewarm and indifferent as to religion, were melted into
repentance, and frequented constantly and conscientiously
these religious meetings. By this means, as two flints clash-
ing together will strike out fire, so the zeal of one Christian
fired and inflamed another. Insomuch that the greatest care of
Brousson and the other preachers was that their meetings
might not be too numerous nor public, lest the faithful should
be exposed unto persecution. But the news of these religious
assemblies made a very great noise not only in the Cévennes
and Lower Languedoc but in all parts of the kingdom, and the
godly were very much edified and confirmed by them.

COURAGEOUS MARTYR

No survey of Brousson's life and ministry, however
brief, is complete without his martyrdom at Montpellier
on 4 November 1698. Quick's account is well attested
and profoundly moving:

My author informs me (who was an eye-witness of his
martyrdom) that he carried it like a true Christian, of an
invincible spirit, one who triumphed over death. There were
near twenty-thousand persons present to see him die, most of
the nobles of the city and country, besides abundance of
foreigners. He prayed earnestly, with his eyes and hands
lifted up to heaven all the way as he was going unto execu-
tion, nor did he take notice of any person till he came unto the
scaffold, his heart and thoughts being wholly taken up with

his approaching change. The mildness and courage with which he ascended up the scaffold is not to be expressed. Though as he passed by them the people wept and groaned, bitterly lamenting the hard fate of a person of such eminent merit and piety, yet you might read the inward calmness of his soul in his smiling looks and cheerful countenance.

He gave his watch unto the Captain of the Count of Broglie's Guards and his cloak to one of the Intendant's messengers who had waited upon him during his imprisonment. Upon the scaffold he made a speech unto the people but no one could be edified by it. For the drummers of the Regiment of Guards did all beat an alarm as soon as he began to speak. M. Brousson having ended with his auditors prepareth himself for death. He putteth off his own clothes to his shirt, yielded both his hands and feet to be fastened to the wheel, and whilst they were tying them up, "'Tis a comfort to me", said he, "that my death hath some resemblance with that of my Lord." The spokes of the wheels were struck into the rands in form of a St Andrew's cross. Being in this posture they pronounce again his final sentence on him which undoubtedly surprised that vast crowd of auditors, if it did not M. Brousson, for he was thereby ordered to be strangled to death, before he was broken on the wheel. This was an unexpected favour. God doth sometimes mollify the hearts of lions. He would not suffer the bloody papists to let out all their rage and cruelty upon His servant.

The executioner having fastened him, went down the scaffold, and being just under the holy martyr, when he had half strangled him, the [metal bar] brake in his hand, so that M. Brousson came to himself again and fell a praying. The

[47]

*Abbé Camarignain hearing him call upon God, came near
unto him [to encourage repentance]. M. Brousson seeing
him [but rejecting the suggestion] said, "May God
Almighty, sir, reward your great charity towards me, and
grant us this mercy, that we may see each other's face in
Paradise!" These were the last words that he was heard to
speak in this world. When he was dead they immediately
brake him upon the wheel. He was very much lamented by
the sober Papists themselves. And well they might; for if
these things be done in the green tree, what will not be done
in the dry? A man asked the executioner how M. Brousson
died. "If I durst speak it out", said he, "I could say much,
but in short, he died a saint, and sealed the truth which he
had preached with his heart's blood." Yea and the Intendant
Bâsville confessed that he never heard a man talk so excel-
lently as Brousson did...*

*When the news of his martyrdom was brought unto Lau-
sanne in Switzerland, M. Merlat, formerly Pastor of the
church of Saintes in France, but then minister in that city,
preaching upon this sorrowful occasion, declared so many
excellent things concerning this martyr, that the whole
congregation burst into tears.*

NOT THE END
Doubtless disappointed at his inability to publish the
Icones, John Quick must have been further distressed
by news from France and especially the Cévennes
during his last years. In the aftermath of Brousson's
death, the tragic failure of the Camisard insurrection
(1702-4) - largely fought on François Vivens' principles
- must have seemed like the end of the Reformed

churches in France. However, as Quick was departing from this world, God was preparing the 'Huguenot Nehemiah'. His name was Antoine Court, born at Villenueve-de-Berg in 1696. In 1715, the very year Louis XIV died, this teenager from the Vivarais was called of God to revive the Reformed Faith in France. Unlike 'le grand monarque', the God of the Calvinists was not dead! The renewed vision, intrepid labours and organizing genius of Antoine Court were to vindicate everything Claude Brousson had lived and died for - but that is for the equally amazing sequel to a truly glorious though sad and violent story, part of which was first told by 'our English Quick'.

Further reading:

Baird, H. M., *The Huguenots and the Revocation of the Edict of Nantes,* 2 vols (London, 1895).

Baynes, H. S., *The Evangelist of the Desert: Life of Claude Brousson* (London , 1853).

Clifford, A. C., *Calvinus: authentic Calvinism, a clarification* (Norwich, 1996).

Gray, J. G., *The French Huguenots: Anatomy of Courage* (Grand Rapids, 1981).

Heath, R., *The Reformation in France* , 2 vols (London, 1886).

Orna-Ornstein, F., *France: forgotten Mission Field* (Welwyn, 1971).

Quick, J., *Synodicon in Gallia Reformata* (London, 1692).
- *Icones Sacrae Gallicanae* (1700), MS on deposit at Dr Williams's Library, London, DWL 6, 38-39 (50).

Smiles, S., *The Huguenots in France after the Revocation*

of the Edict of Nantes (London, 1875).

3

THE HUGUENOT NEHEMIAH

While many are familiar with the great 'Anglo-American' evangelical awakening of the eighteenth century, too little is known in the English-speaking world of the revival of French Protestantism during the same period. Occurring in significantly more hostile conditions, events in France provided a glorious proof of Christ's words regarding his church: 'the gates of hell shall not prevail against it' (Matt. 16: 18). Indeed, such opposition was never more aptly described than in the case of the sufferings of the French Reformed churches following the Revocation of the Edict of Nantes (1685).

What is more remarkable than the scale and nature of the atrocities committed against the Huguenots is the survival and then revival of the Reformed Faith. Notwithstanding the fact that diabolical persecution had produced widespread abjuration among those who would not, or could not, join the refugees, the last years of the seventeenth century testify to the amazing and heroic fortitude of many remaining pastors, elders and people - men and women, old and young. In the

south of France especially, the threat of imprisonment, torture, the galleys and violent death occasioned extraordinary displays of the grace of God in the midst of sufferings quite unmatched in the history of Christianity.

Dating from 1688, the crescendo of persecution produced a 'charismatic' fanaticism among a largely pastorless people. These prophesyings - in which women and children featured prominently - became a desperate yet deceptive remedy for the oppressed. The courageous return to France of several refugee pastors helped to steady the chaotic situation to some degree. However, despair returned following the martyrdom of the 'apostolic' Claude Brousson, executed at Montpellier on 4 November 1698. While the sufferings of this servant of Christ were immortalized in the hearts and memories of Huguenot people, the years of unchecked persecution took their toll. Even the sanctified human nature of Reformed believers was at breaking point. Thus the early years of the eighteenth-century were disfigured by a resort to the sword known as the Camisard revolt (1702-4). Despite the heroic exploits of 'Roland' Laporte and Jean Cavalier, leaders of about three-thousand of Europe's first guerilla fighters against royal troops more than ten times their number, the insurrection was cruelly put down. The struggle persisted spasmodically, finally ending in 1710. However, King Louis XIV and his ministers were forced to acknowledge that Protestantism was not a spent force, despite all the measures used to exterminate it.

SON OF CALVIN

Even the most optimistic Huguenot could not have predicted the 'miracle' of 1715. In the very year of the king's death, a teenager from the Vivarais (modern Ardèche) was stirred at the prospect of restoring French Protestantism. He was indeed the Huguenot Nehemiah. Born at Villeneuve-de-Berg (about 20 km west of Montelimar) on 17 May, 1696, Antoine Court was destined to accomplish great things for God. His father dying when he was four years old, Antoine was blessed with a tender-hearted mother of strong Protestant convictions. At her knees he was taught the Word of God. His convictions were reinforced by the account of Brousson's martyrdom and the exploits of the Camisards.

Like many Protestant children, Antoine was compelled to attend the local Jesuit school. Though young in years, he abhorred the Mass, the symbol of Rome's priestly power and cruelty. Since he was the only Protestant scholar at the school, the others ganged up against him. Antoine was laughed at, spat upon and stoned. As he went home, the Catholic boys shouted "Ha! Ha! eldest son of Calvin!" On one occason, four of them went to his house to force him to attend Mass. Despite their combined attempts to drag him from the stair-rails, Antoine stubbornly shook them off.

Since the Huguenot temples had been demolished at the Revocation, believers gathered by night in remote woods and rocky ravines for Reformed worship. Young Antoine was anxious to attend these secret assemblies of the 'desert church'. One evening, when his mother set out for the meeting, Antoine was determined to follow her. Reprimanded for leaving the house, he replied, "I follow you mother and I wish you to permit me to go where you go. I know that you go to pray to God, and will you refuse me the favour of going to do so with you?" Moved to tears, his mother warned him of the dangers involved. Too young and weak to walk the whole journey, a man in the group hoisted Antoine on to his shoulders and carried him the rest of the way.

Rather than violate his conscience, Antoine refused to 'pay' his way to higher education at a nearby Jesuit college by attending the Mass. While others encouraged him to pursue a trade, he had a thirst for divine truth. Besides the Bible, Antoine's convictions and experience were deepened by reading books by the great Huguenot pastor Charles Drelincourt (1595-1669) and the famous Puritan Richard Baxter (1615-91). The Baxter work was *La voix de Dieu*, a translation of the popular *Call to the Unconverted* (1658). At the age of seventeen, Antoine Court's abilities and zeal were becoming more apparent. He began to read the Bible at the assemblies. On one occasion he began to preach, much to the acceptance of the hearers. Encouraged to exercise his gift more widely, Court was determined to minister to the afflicted Protestants. A naturally anxious mother became willing to release her son for God's service when Court quoted Christ's words, 'Whoever loves father and mother more than me, is not worthy of me' (Matt. 10: 37).

Commencing an itinerant ministry, Court preached

throughout Languedoc and Dauphiné. Despite dangers from spies, priests and dragoons, Court and other preachers ministered to the assemblies. Making his way to Marseille, he managed to penetrate the royal galleys. Without being detected, Court secretly ministered to the hundreds of Huguenot galley slaves. His activities becoming known, he was hotly pursued by spies. He escaped to the mountains of the Cévennes and the Vivarais, gathering large 'desert' congregations wherever he went. This relentless activity took its toll on the young man's health. During enforced rest, Court reflected on measures to revive the Reformed churches of France. Although he was only nineteen years old, having received little formal education and already being hunted by the priests and soldiers, Court was resolute. Looking back on this time, he wrote: "Young as I was, I yet foresaw all the terrible consequences of such a choice; but the firm persuasion that God would watch over me and grant me his protection so long as I did not render myself unworthy of it, confirmed my resolution. It seemed to me that nothing could be too dear to sacrifice for a church for which the Son of God had yielded up his life on the accursed tree, and nothing more glorious for me than to lose mine for his sake."

As Court evaluated the recent past, he was convinced that the interests of French Protestantism had not been well served by either the 'military' or 'fanatical' options. Following in the footsteps of Claude Brousson, he believed that obedience to the Word of God and trust in divine providence was the only way to restore the Reformed churches. Thus with a clear vision, a unique organising genius and incomparable zeal, Court dedicated himself to the work of God. Gathering a group of preachers around him, Court presided over the first synod of the Reformed churches since the national synod of Loudun (1659) - the last to be held before the Revocation. Thus Court succeeded the illustrious Jean Daillé (1594-1670). This new synod was held on 21 August 1715 at Montèze near Monoblet (in the vicinity of Nîmes), just ten days before Louis XIV expired at Versailles! After prayer, Court proposed the reorganizing of the scattered sheep of the Lord. This involved the restoration of the presbyterial discipline of the Reformed churches. Elders were appointed from among those present and regulations drawn up. They reaffirmed the *Confession of Faith* (1559) and authorized the use of Drelincourt's *Catechism* (1642). The preachers were then charged to go forth and stir up the people, especially those who had abjured. Measures were also proposed to discourage the prophesyings and silence the prophetesses. A sacred poignancy belongs to this event, not least because most of those present including Etienne Arnaud were to gain a martyr's crown.

DESERT PASTOR
The youthful Court seems to have been the most active of the preachers. During all weathers and battling against fatigue and sometimes ill-health, his intrepid labours were astonishing. Between one desert meeting and the next, often attended by thousands of worshippers, Court moved swiftly from place to place. Sometimes he came close to capture. When preparing a

sermon in a wood near Nîmes, the sound of soldiers sent him hurriedly up a tree until the danger was passed. On another occasion, hiding beneath a dungheap was the only way to evade the dragoons. Once he was staying with a friend when the house was surrounded by troops. While his friend went to bed pretending to be ill, Court hid in the narrow space between the bedstead and the wall. On bursting into the house, the soldiers examined every likely hiding place except the gap behind the bed! Clearly, as Court himself believed, God's amazing providence was at work.

After serving as a preacher for three years, Court was ordained as a pastor. His old friend, the preacher Pierre Corteiz had received ordination in Zurich. Corteiz then ordained Court at a ceremony held in the Vaunage on the night of 21 November 1718. He was now authorized with the authority of the synod to exercise all the functions of the ministry. Redoubling his energies in the Lord's work, Court was anxious to nourish the faith of the people with sound literature. "Our need of books is very great," he wrote to a friend abroad. After the Revocation, the authorities had seized and burned Protestant Bibles, Psalters, catechisms and other books. Piles were consigned to the flames in every town. Louis XV perpetuated the same policy and immense piles were again destroyed. Refugees in the Netherlands, Switzerland and England responded generously to meet the need. Besides Bibles, Psalters and catechisms, devotional works by Drelincourt, the great Jean Claude (1619-87) and others were sent into France.

Court also saw the importance of theological education for the preachers. When applicants were approved - "good, virtuous men, full of zeal for the cause of truth", as he wrote to Pierre Durand (martyred in 1732) - they had to be well trained. Since the Genevese feared the wrath of France, Court could not depend on the academy there. He therefore resorted to a more basic approach. "I have often pitched my professor's chair in a torrent underneath a rock," he wrote. "The sky was our roof, and the leafy branches thrown out from the crevices in the rock overhead, were our canopy." Based on the French Reformed Confession (drawn up chiefly by Calvin), a rigorous theological programme included an exacting homiletic training. "When the more advanced students were required to preach, they mounted a particular place, where a pole had been set across some rocks in the ravine, and which for the time served for a pulpit. And when they had delivered themselves, the others were requested by turns to express themseves freely upon the subject of the sermon which they had heard."

While funds offered by the faithful were scarce, young men were never wanting to supply the places of the martyred preachers. Court himself shared the austere conditions of his brethren. His labours were prodigious. During a two-month period, he visited thirty-one churches in Lower Languedoc and the Cévennes. Travelling over three hundred miles (480 km), he held 'desert' assemblies, preaching and administering the sacraments. By the year 1729, there were over 200,000 confessing Protestants in Languedoc alone. Though secretly governed, there were forty churches in

Languedoc, eighteen in the Cévennes, twelve in Lozère and forty-two in the Vivarais. In all, one hundred and twenty churches had been re-established, each with an eldership and supported by a provincial synod. Despite the cruel oppression of new royal edicts against the Huguenots, the movement spread to other parts of France. Dauphiné in the south-east, Béarn and Guienne in the south-west, Saintonge and Poitou in the west, and Normandy and Picardy in the far north felt the heaven-blest influence of Antoine Court and his brethren.

SEMINARY PROFESSOR

For some time, Court cherished the possibility of setting up a ministerial academy in a less vulnerable situation. The providence of God was to make this a reality. After marrying a young Huguenot woman in 1722, Court's home at Uzès became the base for his activities. To avoid jeopardizing his ministry, he visited his wife and three children secretly. Suspicions were aroused in the neighbourhood since Mme Court was known as a woman of godly reputation. When the new commandant of Uzès made searching enquiries about the woman's husband, Court acted to remove them from danger. Making arrangements for them to escape to Geneva, Court's family reached the city in April 1729. Continuing to preach in Languedoc, Court became seriously ill. Utterly exhausted and anxious for his family, he made a hazardous journey to join them in Geneva. This development enabled Court to realise his objective. Despite the expostulations of his brethren - who even began to doubt his courage (!), Court was determined to serve the cause of God in ways they failed to envisage. Eventually settling with his family in Lausanne, he opened a seminary there. Until his death thirty years later, Court prepared the zealous and single-minded youths of Languedoc and the Vivarais for ministry and often martyrdom in the service of Christ and his suffering saints. The number of itinerant pastors steadily grew. By 1756 there were forty-eight pastors at work with twenty-two probationary preachers and students.

The restored churches were spared neither periodic persecution nor internal dissensions. Asked to mediate in a case of pastoral misconduct, Court made a precarious journey to Languedoc in 1744. Still with a price on his head, his return was hailed with immense rejoicing. Preaching to vast crowds wherever he went, Court remained in France for about a month. Despite excessive heat and wearisome travel, and never without danger, he saw widespread evidence of the blessing of God. Arriving at a prearranged location near Montpellier well after midnight, Court was greeted by a large and enthusiastic assembly. "I dismounted," he wrote, "put on my gown, ascended the pulpit [a portable device used on such occasions], and preached with as much power as though I had come straight from my study." Near Sauzet (20 km south-east of Anduze), nearly twenty-thousand people assembled. At this national synod, the pastoral schism was resolved. When the reconciled parties embraced one another, the whole assembly broke forth into a psalm. Court later preached to nearly seven-thousand souls in a grove near Alès. "The scene under the tents was beautiful," he recorded, "there was great rejoicing when I appeared in the pulpit." Returning to Lausanne in October 1744, Court wrote: 'I have left the Protestants full of zeal, and in a state incomparably better than at any time since the Revocation."

Antoine Court's wife died in 1755. Keenly feeling his loss, this intrepid servant of Christ laboured on. He died on the 15 June 1760. Brilliantly followed in the seminary by his son Court Gebelin, Court's acknowledged successor among the churches was the equally remarkable Paul Rabaut (1718-94). Under his wise and zealous leadership, the restored Reformed churches of France became established. Notwithstanding occasional continuing persecution, they finally obtained religious liberty in the Edict of Toleration (1787), granted by Louis XVI on the eve of the French Revolution (1789). Truly, the 'gates of hell' did not prevail against the true church. On the contrary, the royal despotism that had oppressed it perished in the divine judgement of the Reign of Terror. Indeed, Court and his comrades in the faith proved repeatedly, that none can withstand Him who declared, "All power is given unto me in heaven and on earth" (Matt. 28: 18).

Further reading:

Baird, H. M.,*The Huguenots and the Revocation of the Edict of Nantes* (London, 1895).
Clifford, A. C., *Calvinus: authentic Calvinism, a clarification* (Norwich, 1996).

Grant, A. J., *The Huguenots* (London, 1934).

Gray, J. G., *The French Huguenots: Anatomy of Courage* (Grand Rapids, 1981).

Gwynn, R. D., *Huguenot Heritage* (London, 1985).

Hugues, E., *Antoine Court Histoire de la Restauration du Protestantisme en France au XVIIIe siècle* (Paris, 1872).

- (ed), *Mémoires d'Antoine Court* (Paris, 1885).

Orna-Ornstein, F., *France...Forgotten Mission Field* (Welwyn, 1971).

Prestwich, M., (ed), *International Calvinism, 1541-1715* (Oxford, 1985).

Smiles, S., *The Huguenots in France after the Revocation of the Edict of Nantes* (London, 1875).

Tylor, C.,*The Camisards: a sequel to 'The Huguenots of the Seventeenth Century'* (London, 1893).

THE HUGUENOT CROSS AND ITS MEANING

The cross was made popular by a Protestant jeweller from Nîmes in the late seventeenth century. It became associated with the Huguenots and their sufferings in the post-revocation period. In time, the following interpretations became attached to it:

1. A variant of the Maltese cross was the basis of an insignia - the Order of the Holy Spirit - awarded by the French kings to soldiers and statesmen.

2. The Huguenots claimed the symbol (with slight variation) as Frenchmen and as 'soldiers of Christ'.

3. The four branches of the cross became emblems of the four Gospels.

4. The eight points of the cross came to symbolize the Beatitudes (Matthew 5:1-12) - marks of the true people of God.

5. The crown of thorns symbolizes the Huguenots' identification with Christ in all their persecutions and martyrdoms.

6. The four heart-shapes between the crown of thorns and the centre of the cross depict the hearts of God's people centred upon Christ alone for salvation.

7. The dove speaks of the Holy Spirit, the strength and comfort of God's elect in their pilgrimage to the glory everlasting.